10
to G
the New Testament
A Teenager's Guide

Jim Auer

LIGUORI
PUBLICATIONS

One Liguori Drive
Liguori, Missouri 63057-9999
(314) 464-2500

Imprimi Potest:
James Shea, C.SS.R.
Provincial, St. Louis Province
The Redemptorists

Imprimatur:
Monsignor Maurice F. Byrne
Vice Chancellor, Archdiocese of St. Louis

ISBN 0-89243-342-6
Library of Congress Catalog Card Number: 90-64270

Cover design by Pam Hummelsheim

ABOUT THE AUTHOR

Jim Auer teaches in a Catholic junior high school. He's a consultant
for Liguori Publications, the author of many "Under 21" articles in
Liguorian magazine, and the author of many books for Liguori
including *10 Good Reasons To Be a Catholic* and *10 Tough Issues
for Teenagers.* He and his wife and two children live in Cincinnati,
Ohio.

CONTENTS

INTRODUCTION

It's the year two thousand and something. A team of religious leaders and scientists have perfected supernatural fiber optics, which enables telephone conversations between earth and heaven. Imagine this one. It's not as wild as it may seem....

GOD   God here, thanks for waiting. Did you like the music while you were on hold? Pretty nice stuff, I thought.

YOU   Uh, sure, but we have that down here too.

GOD   Not the same. You heard a choir of angels, *live,* just for you, not that recorded elevator stuff.

YOU   I didn't know angels did all that.

GOD   I made angels versatile. What can I do for you?

YOU   It's, uh…about the Bible.

GOD   One of the best things we ever did.

YOU   "We?" Who is "we"?

GOD   People and I. I love to let my creatures in on things. Surely you must have picked this up. For example, you get to help more people — I *know* you've noticed that. So when it came to writing the Bible, I let some people in on the job. Turned out really well.

YOU   Right. It's wonderful.

GOD   How would you know?

YOU   Well, I've…heard people say it's wonderful.

GOD   But you don't exactly know from hours of personal Bible reading.

YOU   Right. That's the problem I was calling about.

GOD   I know.

YOU   You do?

GOD   I'm God. Goes with the territory. But tell me anyway. I like it when people talk to me. Wish they'd do it more.

YOU   Okay, if the Bible is the Word of…You, and it's full of all kinds of truth and inspirational stuff, then why… I don't know how to say this but…

GOD   Why doesn't every verse reach out and make you want to read it more than anything else in the world? Why isn't the Bible flashier and glitzier?

YOU   That's it exactly.

GOD   I don't like a lot of showboat stuff. That's for rock stars and professional wrestlers. I'm a little quieter. So is the Bible. Let me ask you this: Is a steamy day in July a good time to read *A Christmas Carol*?

YOU   Of course not.

GOD   Bingo.

YOU   I don't think I understand.

GOD   A good book deserves the right surroundings. The Bible more so than any other. That doesn't mean you have to wait for a perfect time and place that will only happen once every ten years, which is about how often some people read the Bible. Just give the Bible a chance. Choose a quiet time. And tune in to what you're going to do before you start reading.

YOU   Okay.

GOD   Another thing — ever go to one of those 3-D movies?

YOU   You mean where you have to wear those funny-looking glasses, and when you do, you see the movie in three dimensions?

GOD   Right. And if you don't have the glasses?

YOU	Then it looks just like an ordinary movie.
GOD	Lots of people read the Bible without the right glasses. Seems like an ordinary book then.
YOU	I don't get it. What are the right glasses?
GOD	Faith. If you read the Bible with faith, you see what's really there, and it can have an effect on you. Read it without faith and it's a collection of familiar stories and nice sayings.
YOU	But some parts are hard to understand.
GOD	They weren't intended to be. They were actually very clear to the people who first read them and heard them. Sometimes you need to get into the culture of the times and the mind of my colleagues, the human authors, to understand it fully. In that respect, it's a little like reading Shakespeare.
YOU	Any suggestions?
GOD	There are some decent books out. But don't make the mistake of reading a book about the Bible and then not reading the Bible. That's like reading a review of a terrific movie but never going to see the movie. You miss out on the real thing.
YOU	And the popcorn.
GOD	Popcorn was one of my better ideas. A much better idea than squash, for example.
YOU	Would it be okay to eat popcorn while I'm reading the Bible?
GOD	No problem. You can read the Bible while you're eating popcorn too. Go easy on the salt.

CHAPTER ONE

It's the Gospel Truth

I have a radical suggestion.

It's so radical it may take me awhile to work up to it. I don't have what it takes to come right out with it. I'm really pretty sure it will work, but...

Okay, I'll admit it, I'm chicken. Everybody's a little chicken now and then. Just yesterday after school, for example, I talked with a guy I teach. In the eyes of most girls, he would qualify as a total hunk, a dream date. We talked about how to deal with his absolute terror of calling this girl he likes and asking her out. Fear of rejection.

Well, I'm afraid of rejection too, so I'll work up to this radical idea gradually.

In the meantime let's talk gospels. That's not too threatening. We can handle this because we know most of it already, right? Matthew, Mark, Luke, and John — they are the first four books of the New Testament. They tell about the life of Jesus. Piece of religious cake.

Oft-told Tales

We all know about the life of Jesus, right?

Actually, that's the problem. We think the gospels are intended to tell us how Jesus was born in Bethlehem, grew up, then traveled around Palestine working miracles and saying inspirational things. Finally, he was put to death on the cross and rose again on the third day.

It's a great story and we're glad it happened, but we've heard it before. We know how it comes out. Even many of the details along the way are kind of familiar. For example, as soon as one of the gospels says, "There was a blind man," we know that Jesus will cure him a few verses later. So we figure — why read something that tells us what we already more or less know?

Once again our problem is thinking that the gospels were written to give us basic information about the life of Jesus. Our problem is thinking of the gospels as minibiographies filled with facts that prove Jesus was a real person who went around talking about love and doing good things for people a couple of thousand years ago.

If that's what Matthew, Mark, Luke, and John had in mind when they wrote, none of them was very good at it. If you judge by the standards of biography, the gospels aren't very good at all.

Confused by Facts

Only Matthew and Luke say anything at all about the birth of Jesus. The other two begin his life story with Jesus as a young man. Except for one single incident in Luke, the thirty years between his birth and his public ministry are a total blank. Things that would be standard in any decent biography, like the death of Jesus' foster father, Joseph, are left out.

On top of that, the evangelists can't seem to get their facts straight. In Matthew, Jesus gives his famous sermon from a mountain. When Luke tells the story, he says Jesus spoke from a "level place" *after* he had come down from the mountain. They seem to be talking about the same incident because both mention the beatitudes. One small problem here too: Matthew gives us eight beatitudes; Luke gives us four.

Why? Because Luke didn't take good notes and would have gotten a fifty on a Bible test? Because either Matthew or Luke flunked geography and couldn't tell a mountain from a plain?

Of course not. It's because the evangelists just weren't into stuff like getting times and places and the order of events straight.

Let's say you write a paper about the life of Abraham Lincoln and your history teacher says, "Your paper gives some outstanding insights into Lincoln and what his life meant, but your presentation of historical facts is…well, pretty sloppy." In that case your paper has some similarity to the gospels. The gospel is not a strict biography.

Facts and Faith

It's not that the evangelists were sloppy writers. In different ways each was a genius. It just takes us awhile to tune in to what they were trying to accomplish when they put "The Jesus Story" into words.

A verse from the Gospel according to John tells us flat out what the evangelists had in mind. It wasn't a religious history lesson or information to study so you can pass a religion course. It wasn't to prove that Jesus really lived.

> But these [signs] are written that you may [come to] believe that Jesus is the Messiah, the Son of God, and that through this belief you may have life in his name.
>
> (John 20:31)

In other words there are two people actively involved in the gospels. The first is Jesus and the second is you. Sure, scholars can study the heck out of the ancient manuscripts and come up with marvelous conclusions, and that's a good deal because we often need their help, BUT…

…that's not why Matthew, Mark, Luke, and John took up gospel writing. *You are!*

And not so you can pass a high-school or CCD or PSR Bible quiz. You can be a confirmed atheist and pass a Bible quiz, if you study. That's no problem.

Three words or ideas in that verse from John give the reason for all the words in the gospels: *you, faith,* and *life.*

Gospel Similarities

This all brings me pretty close to my radical suggestion, and I'm tempted to come out with it right now. But I'm still a little scared. I'll get to it in just a few more minutes.

In the meantime let's talk a little about how the gospels got to be gospels. That's a little safer and pretty interesting.

Let's say you sit down and read all four gospels straight through. I don't recommend that, but if you did, you'd probably start with Matthew, since it's placed first in the New Testament. Then you'd get to Mark, and about halfway through Mark, you'd realize that you're reading some incidents for the second time. Not everything — a lot of Mark would be new material. But some things would be very familiar, just told with different details added or with some details missing. And some verses would seem almost identical to what you had read in Matthew.

Then you'd get to Luke and the same thing would happen all over again: a few things almost identical, others told with amazing similarity, and a good bit of material that you hadn't read at all in the first two gospels (like the famous Christmas story).

Finally, you'd get to the Gospel according to John. After a chapter or two you'd think, "This is a different ball game." You'd think so even more strongly when you finished.

Since John is so different, we're going to leave it aside for a moment and concentrate on Matthew, Mark, and Luke.

The Synoptic Gospels

Matthew, Mark, and Luke are so similar that they are called the synoptic gospels. *Synoptic* means looking at something from the same viewpoint, or sort of drawing it all together, a synopsis.

The authors of these three gospels didn't sit next to one another in a course called "Introduction to Gospel Writing." They wrote at different times and in different places. Scripture scholars figure there must have been an earlier document, not an actual gospel but a collection of the stories and sayings of Jesus. That document has been long lost by now, but the authors of Matthew, Mark, and Luke must have had it to work from when they put together their gospels.

Actually, that's a supersimple version of how Matthew, Mark, and Luke came to be and why they are similar yet different. Most introductions to the New Testament have a full explanation if you'd like to find out more.

Since the synoptic gospels have so many similarities, it might seem like a great idea to combine them. Leave out all the repetition and just put in the items that are brand-new from one gospel to the next. Advertising would have a ball with this:

"Introducing the revolutionary new *Super Gospel!* Why read those same synoptic items over again when you go through Matthew, Mark, and Luke? We've combined the best of all three into one convenient, streamlined gospel, perfect for the busy lifestyle of the nineties. Order your *Super Gospel* now! Just send $7.95 plus $15.50 for postage and handling...."

Actually, it's been tried (not with advertising like that though). But it's not a great idea. The following example may help show why.

Three Portraits

Suppose you take three photographic portraits of someone you admire very much. One shows the person in a gentle, happy, loving mood. You can almost feel the peace and harmony flowing from the face on the photo. A second portrays the same person in a very serious mood. Strong determination, maybe even a little anger, shows on the face. The third portrait features the person in a wonderfully crazy mood. Excitement with life and maybe a little delightful mischief are written all over his or her face.

Now imagine that someone offers to take a computerized scan of each portrait and combines them into a computerized composite that will be a mixture of some elements of each portrait. Bad idea, right? The wonderful uniqueness of each of the original three portraits would be lost.

Something like that would happen if we tried to combine the synoptic gospels into one. Now I don't mean that Matthew shows Jesus as gentle and loving, Mark paints him as determined and angry, and Luke shows him as excited and mischievous.

You have to spend time getting familiar with these gospels to see this, but they give us three wonderfully different portraits of Jesus. Like the three portraits in our example, they are all true and real, but they're different.

Something Radical

Well, that's it. I guess I could try to give you a tiny capsule of Matthew, Mark, and Luke, but each would be too short and too simple. It would be like trying to describe baseball as a game where you hit a ball with a piece of wood and then run around in a circle. That's sort of correct, but it's also very primitive.

So that leaves you with the ball — or rather the gospels — in your hands. Which brings me to the radical suggestion I backed away from earlier. All this talk about gospels has psyched me up for it.

Read a gospel — *an entire gospel!*

I told you it was radical. But please don't put it on a list of "Religious Stuff I Might Do When I Get Really Old." Give it a shot.

As for which of the synoptic gospels is the best one to start with, I've heard nominations for all three. You choose. And you don't have to read it all at one time. Divide it up, but not into a hundred sections stretched out over a couple of decades. A chapter a day is a pretty good pace.

Before you begin each time, say a short simple prayer like "Jesus, let me really see you in what I read" or "Holy Spirit, point out something I need to hear in these words."

That makes it even more radical, doesn't it? In fact, you have to be pretty brave to say a prayer like that and mean it because you can be sure God will answer. God will show you something.

And when that happens and you take it in, the three key words of why the gospels were written will be coming together once again — *you, faith,* and *life.*

And now we close with a final radical suggestion — start today!

CHAPTER TWO

A Brief Course in Ultimate Reality

"Those are the hour's top stories…details and additional film at eleven. And now we go to Hal Morrison for this evening's edition of Ultimate Reality. Hal."

"Thanks, Christy. Today we're outside the main entrance of the new All Seasons Mall, a sprawling complex of one hundred ninety stores. The Grand Opening is in progress and there is excitement all around. It seems like a great place to ask several interesting people our daily question: "What is the Ultimate Reality?" How about you, sir? Are you familiar with channel nine's *Ultimate Reality* segment?"

"Oh, sure. I catch it a lot. I'd love to comment."

"Terrific. In your opinion, what *is* Ultimate Reality?"

"P and L, Hal. Good old P and L."

"P and L?"

"Yeah, profit and loss. You make a buck, you lose a buck. But if you're good, you make two for every one you lose. That's what it's all about."

"Interesting opinion, and one I'm sure shared by many. Thank you. And you, ma'am. What do you think is the Ultimate Reality?"

"Syncro-cosmic Omnilism. It's brand-new, Hal, but it's ultimate — definitely ultimate."

"I haven't heard of Syncro..."

"It's generated by a computer program. Compatible with IBM, Apple, and all major systems. And it's user-friendly. You plug in the major ideas of all the great religions, all the big thinkers — anything you think is important."

"That's incredible."

"It really is, Hal. This program handles everything — Plato, Buddhism, Hinduism, Christianity, socialism, New Age crystal power, top forty song lyrics."

"And then what happens?"

"The program weaves everything together and gives you a complete printout of the whole homogenized package. That's Syncro-cosmic Omnilism."

"Thank you. I'm sure a lot of our viewers will look into this. Time for one final opinion. Sir, your Ultimate Reality?"

"Stuff."

"Stuff?"

"Stuff. Think about it, Hal. Stuff is all around us. We can't get away from it. Now *that's* Ultimate Reality!"

What Is Real?

I don't think any station or network is doing a segment like that, but I'd love to see it if one did. If there are any news producers reading this booklet, you're welcome to use the idea.

What would *you* answer?

We don't think about the question too often. We're usually too tied up with the nuts and bolts of our daily lives. Some of those nuts and bolts are more important than others — a SAT test is more important than this evening's sitcom, for example. But neither deals with the question, "What's behind it all?"

Once in a while that question crosses our thoughts. Maybe the

17

death of someone close brings it to mind. Maybe a friend gets into a bunch of strange but intriguing ideas, shares them, and makes us wonder how much of it might be real. Even though we prefer music or pizza over philosophy, we start wondering, "What *is* real?"

A Familiar Answer

Unfortunately, we Christians know the answer. The unfortunate part is that we've known it for too long, for too much of our lives.

When we were young, in religion class or CCD/PSR or Sunday school, the teacher said, "Jesus died for us and saved us from our sins." And we said, "Okay."

The teacher said, "Jesus was a human being like us, but he was also God. He is one of the Persons of the Blessed Trinity, along with God the Father and God the Holy Spirit." And we said, "Okay."

The teacher said, "Jesus is still with us. We can talk to him. And we can celebrate his presence among us at the Eucharist." And we said, "Okay."

We heard it when we were six and again when we were eight and again when we were ten, and so forth.

It sort of got old before it had a chance to be exciting.

So today if someone says, "We're going to have a séance. We're going to *contact the other dimension and find out what's over there!*" it sounds pretty fascinating.

And yet we Christians have been able to do that all the time.

Something Real

The writer of John's Gospel lived in somewhat the same situation. It had been several decades since Jesus. There had been time to think not just about what Jesus said and did but about who he was and is.

And looking back, Jesus seemed pretty ordinary — a man, a carpenter.

And yet he couldn't have been just a man. He was the Messiah, meaning God's anointed one, yes, but he was even more than that. He changed things, radically changed things, even though they might look the same on the outside.

But how? And what was the difference? And how do we become a part of it all?

These are all questions of Ultimate Reality. And John's Gospel is rich with answers.

The answers are not written in the plain factual style we're used to, so it's possible to read the Gospel and come away feeling, "That sounds heavy, but I don't get it."

It takes a little work — the really worthwhile kind, the kind that leaves you thinking, "I see things differently now and it's wonderful!"

And it takes faith, faith that we are actually reading words "written from the 'other dimension.' "

They are, of course. They are John's words and God's words at the same time.

If we don't believe that, then the Bible is just an ancient book, and we might as well pick up a good mystery novel instead.

Reality According to John

Hundreds of thousands of words have been written about John's Gospel. We have perhaps nine hundred left in this chapter. So you can safely guess that this will not exactly be a complete study of John's Gospel. But maybe we can open the door an inch or two; then it will be up to you.

Your Bible will probably have three major section headings in John's Gospel. The first very small section (John 1:1-18) is called the Prologue. The second (John 1:19—12:50) is called the Book of Signs. The third (John 13:1—20:31) is called the Book of Glory. Chapter Twenty-one (often called the Epilogue) seems to be an addition, attached sometime later to the original Gospel.

In one way the Prologue says it all. "In the beginning was the Word, and the Word was with God, and the Word was God....And the Word became flesh and made his dwelling among us, and we saw his glory, the glory as of the Father's only Son, full of grace and truth" (1:1, 14).

Today we have an official term for this: the *Incarnation.* It's a shame the word sounds kind of cold and technical to some people because the reality is absolutely breathtaking: God became a human being!

He didn't just make us, didn't just give us stuff, didn't just smile at us from "way up there"...he *became one of us!*

That's going pretty far.

Is God a little crazy or what?

In a way, yes. People in love do crazy things, things that don't make any sense at all except that they're in love.

Book of Signs

John gives us exactly that explanation in the verse you some-times see on homemade signs along the highway or on banners at sporting events.

> For God so loved the world that he gave his only Son, so that everyone who believes in him might not perish but might have eternal life.
>
> (John 3:16)

Too far out, too good to be true?

That's what many people thought and still think. So John gives us the Book of Signs, things Jesus said and did to show that this is real, this is true, this is what everything is all about.

This is Ultimate Reality!

It begins with the miracle at Cana, where Jesus changed water into wine. Look at the spectacular mix in that story!

Only God can take water and make it into wine just by thinking it so. (And it was rather good wine, according to the headwaiter's comment.)

So we have a miracle, a proof that Jesus is God. That's the "heavenly" part of the mix.

Now look at the "earthly" or ordinary part: a young couple's wedding reception kept on going without embarrassment to them. A beautiful mix of God and humanity.

Exactly what John told us in the Prologue: "And the Word became flesh" (1:14).

Book of Glory

The events in the Book of Glory, beginning with Chapter Thirteen, certainly didn't look glorious at the time. Without faith, they still don't. Jesus suffers — horribly, unreasonably, unjustly — and dies.

Today some crucifixes look almost decorative. The gruesome reality of a Roman crucifixion would probably have made most of us throw up.

And yet Jesus calls this his hour of glory (see John 17:1-5).

You can kind of pick up the idea that God doesn't always think along the same lines as we do.

It's glorious because in the Crucifixion Jesus takes all the awfulness that is in this world, puts it on himself, and changes it. He doesn't take it away. He changes the meaning of it. He makes it possible for us to overcome it, to actually use it as a steppingstone leading to where he is about to return — to the Father in heaven.

Sin is still here. Tragedy is still here. But they don't have to beat us anymore.

There's more good news in Chapter Fourteen. Another great mystery and good news at the same time. We are not alone. We have very special help, a third Person, the Spirit, whom the Father will send to us.

A Spectacular Mystery

The Holy Trinity. Like the Incarnation, no way would we have ever come to this on our own. The smartest, holiest people could have thought for a million years and never come up with this. God is a threesome, a Trinity of separate Persons so completely united in love that they are one.

That's not ever going to fit in your brain. In this life, at least, you'll never get a little light bulb over your head and say, "*Now* I get it, now I understand how there can be three Persons in one God!"

A mystery. But what a spectacular mystery.

We sometimes have difficulties though with mysteries like that. We've already mentioned one problem. We've heard them so often without really thinking about them or we heard them before we were even able to think about them.

But what also bothers many of us is that if we really buy them, if we really mean it when we say "I believe," we can't just stop there. We have to do something. We have to change our lives.

If we *truly believe* that Jesus is both God and human, that he came from the Father, died to save us, returned to the Father, and sent us the Spirit, and that this all happened because God is crazily in love with us, we can't just say, "That's interesting."

We have to decide to be a part of it or not.

And that is exactly one of the major themes all through John's Gospel — the need to decide for or against Jesus.

John hopes we will decide for Jesus — that's why he wrote his Gospel.

Now Jesus did many other signs in the presence of [his] disciples that are not written in this book. But these are written that you may [come to] believe that Jesus is the Messiah, the Son of God, and that through this belief you may have life in his name.

(John 20:30-31)

Reading John's Gospel will help us make that decision. And it's a good feeling to be in touch with the Ultimate Reality.

CHAPTER THREE

The Impossible Sequel

It never should have worked — not in a million years.

The odds were impossibly against it. Even if you were addicted to gambling, you wouldn't have risked two bucks on this one.

I'm talking about the story in Luke's sequel.

Sequels are big these days. Any filmmaker who sees something worth milking another time around makes a sequel…and sometimes another and another. By the time you have grandchildren, theaters will be showing *Friday the Thirteenth, Part* XXXIV: Jason Collects Social Security. Or you'll see a gray-haired Rambo wasting all the bad guys who tried to take over the senior citizen center.

Luke's Incredible Sequel

Sequels aren't new. There's a great one that's about nineteen hundred years old. It's in the New Testament and it's called the Acts of the Apostles. It tells an impossible story, a story that didn't have a chance according to the way we usually measure things. It tells the story of the spread of Christianity.

Acts is a sequel because Luke wrote a first volume, which we now call the Gospel according to Luke. In his Gospel, Luke told the Jesus story. A few years later he wrote the Church story, which we now call the Acts of the Apostles.

We grow up knowing this story in a way, sort of, more or less. And sometimes knowing it actually stands in our way. Earlier we talked about the way fantastic things can begin to sound ordinary. We hear about them so often, beginning with childhood, that they get old before they have a chance to be exciting.

In the case of Acts, we grew up with the idea that the apostles started preaching about Jesus and people instantly started believing what they said (apparently people were holier back then), so pretty soon there was this thing called Christianity and everything was religiously cool. And it's all been with us for a long time — so what's the big deal?

It seems like a script that had to be, and these people called early Christians came along and acted it out.

Let's Pretend

Here's an idea. Read Acts and try to pretend you've never heard the story before.

When you do, you'll begin to see how we can say that events in Acts didn't stand a chance, not by the way we usually judge things.

Let's use a comparison. A few years ago some of the richest and smartest businesspeople in the country got together and began a "new" version of something this country usually can't get enough of: professional football. They established the United States Football League.

It had everything going for it: a popular idea; lots of smart, experienced, powerful, and successful businesspeople; some of the most talented, highly paid athletes of the time; millions and millions of investment dollars; and wide publicity.

Three years later…fizzle — bomb — nowhere.

There are tons of similar examples, things that had everything going for them but didn't work out. Or things that hit the sky for a short while and then faded into nothing. (Remember when people literally fought for a Cabbage Patch doll or a ticket to a Beastie Boys concert?)

Compare things like that with what happened in Luke's story in Acts.

Mission Impossible

There's this small group of absolutely ordinary people. They are not especially educated. They have almost no money, very little social power or influence, and they don't even seem to be particularly charming or attractive. By most standards they've got nothing to work with.

Here's their job: to tell people that another ordinary-looking person, a carpenter from a little country town, was actually the Son of God and that he makes all the cosmic, eternal difference in everybody's life.

Even though he died by execution as a common criminal without complaining or trying to do anything to stop it.

After that they had to tell people that the carpenter came back to life. He rose from the tomb where he was buried, appeared here and there to some of his friends for forty days (and apparently had some fun doing so), and then went back to heaven.

Oh, yeah, by the way, because of all this, you have to make some major changes in the way you live, some changes that are going to cost you. If you really buy this package, you're going to take some heat for it.

A tiny group of ordinary, untrained people are going to spread this totally off-the-wall idea *throughout the whole world? This is going to work?*

C'mon, give us a break! The plot in *Attack of the Mushroom People* is more logical than this.

But it happened. Faith in this impossibly wonderful message spread throughout the world. In Acts, Luke tells the story of how it happened during those first few years.

ACTion-packed Adventure

You read most books of the Bible for inspiration, for wisdom. Most are a little difficult to read just for fun. Take Leviticus or Numbers in the Old Testament, for example. They're great books, but it's hard to imagine settling down after a long day and getting lost in a few chapters just to relax.

Acts of the Apostles is different. You can read it just for fun.

The title is both misleading and accurate. It's misleading if you take apostles to mean the original Twelve. They get a brief mention in the first chapter, and that's about it, except for Peter, who had a major role in the first several chapters, and James, who is mentioned a couple of times as bishop of Jerusalem.

But the title is extremely accurate if you take *Acts* to mean "action." Acts was written about nineteen centuries too early for car chases, but it does feature some great courtroom drama, a really super earthquake, a couple of secret plots, a few riots, some jailbreaks and late-night escapes, a storm at sea, and a shipwreck. That's along with minor stuff like a snakebite and a fall from a third-story window.

Luke is a great storyteller. His style isn't Stephen King or S.E. Hinton or Judy Blume. His style is pure Luke. And remember, he wasn't sitting at a typewriter or a word processor in some office in Jerusalem. Working by hand with primitive materials, he couldn't crank out hundreds of words. So he had to make the ones he wrote really count. Even with those limitations, Luke gives us a great variety of literary style.

It's All There

If you're looking for humor, read the account of Peter's escape from prison in Chapter Twelve. Among other things, you'll meet a very sleepy leader of the Church, a very patient angel, and a wonderfully lovable scatterbrained maid named Rhoda. Rhoda does almost everything right — almost! Read Chapter Twelve to see what she forgets. (I can't wait to meet Rhoda when I get to heaven. I've talked about her a couple of times before, and somehow I know her soul is going to float up to mine and say, "Now, look. I can *explain* that!")

For a small but gradually unfolding suspense episode, read Chapter Twenty-three. For more fun, imagine seeing it on film.

To listen in on some intense emotion, read the scene of Paul's farewell to his friends at Miletus in Chapter Twenty (verses 17-38). It's the closest Luke comes to the kind of emotional monologue you might hear on today's soaps.

For pure action-adventure, go with Paul on his final trip (as far as we know) to Rome in Chapters Twenty-seven and Twenty-eight. He makes it, but along the way there's everything except a hijacking.

Outward Expansion

Luke's action in Acts begins in Jerusalem and keeps getting farther away. That's no accident. It serves Luke's whole theme, and he designed it that way.

Luke wants to show the expanding of the Church outward. At the beginning of Acts, the Church is a small group of frightened believers huddled together in a room in Jerusalem. At the end the Church is composed of large communities of believers who are willing to put their lives on the line for Jesus hundreds of miles away.

Here's a brief outline: Chapters One through Seven are set in Jerusalem, with the gospel being preached to people who, like the apostles themselves, were brought up in the Jewish faith.

Chapter Eight moves outward to include Samaritans, who were only partly Jewish, having intermarried with other people. Then we move on to an Ethiopian.

Now this fellow is not Jewish, but he's not completely Gentile either. He represents the people the Jews called "God-fearers" — they believed in the one God of Israel and used Jewish Scriptures, but they did not adopt all the Jewish religious customs and laws.

In Chapter Nine, Luke gives us the story of perhaps the most dramatic reversal of all time: the conversion of Paul on the way to Damascus.

Saul, the Christian-hater and big-time professional persecutor, becomes Paul, the Christian. Paul's conversion paves the way for bringing the gospel further and further outward from Jerusalem because it is he who will lead that missionary effort.

Good News for All

Now you might think Paul's preaching career was a nonstop blazing success right from the start.

Not exactly. Actually, it began with disaster.

For quite a while Paul had everybody mad at him. Many of his fellow Jews considered him a traitor who had defected to the Christian cause. Most Christians didn't trust him because just a short while ago he had tried awfully hard to put them out of business. ("You're one of us now? Yeah…right. Tell us another one.")

At this point many people would have quit, and for a while Paul did go back home to Tarsus to sort things out.

In the meantime full acceptance of the Gentiles comes in Chapters Ten and Eleven, beginning with the baptism of a Roman centurion named Cornelius.

This was upsetting to many of the Jewish Christians. It took awhile even for Peter himself to get the idea that the good news about Jesus was meant for *everybody* — even those rotten awful pagan Romans and those stuck-up intellectual Greeks and… whoever.

Acts 11:9-26 sounds like a low-key, almost by-the-way passage, but it's monumentally significant. The Church is officially established at Antioch, where Jewish converts are joined by many Gentiles. Eventually, Antioch will become a center of Christianity equal to Jerusalem.

Travels With Paul

Paul's three great missionary journeys make up a great deal of the rest of Acts. Luke tells the story of the first journey in Acts 13:1—14:27, the second in Acts 15:36—18:22, and the third in Acts 18:23—21:16.

Following that, he returns to Jerusalem, where he gets into major trouble, spends a good bit of time in prison, and finally demands that his case be tried at the imperial court in Rome so he can get a fair trial. Paul can demand this because, unlike most of the Jews, he was also a Roman citizen. Roman citizenship carried quite a few legal privileges, which Paul often used to his advantage.

The trip to Rome (Acts 27 and 28) was not exactly a peaceful cruise, as we've hinted at before, but Paul makes it. We know he was there for at least two years under house arrest. And there the story stops.

That's disappointing to people who want to know exactly what happened to Paul, but Luke probably intended it to end like that. In the final verse Paul is preaching, the gospel is being spread. Luke is saying that this is the way things are now and this is the way they'll continue to be.

Spirit-led

How did this impossible story actually happen? There's only one explanation. People are not in charge here. God is — specifically the Holy Spirit. The promise to send the Spirit, which Jesus made so eloquently in the Gospel according to John, is fulfilled in Acts. The evidence is right there. A group of frightened believers have become fired-up, take-on-the-world apostles.

Ask the Spirit to be in charge of your reading of Acts too. You'll have even more fun with it when the Spirit guides you, just as the Spirit guided those early believers through the real-life action in Luke's impossible and wonderful sequel.

CHAPTER FOUR

Will the Real Sinners Please Stand Up?

Will all sinners please raise their hands? No, you don't have to say what your sin is, just raise your hand if you are a sinner. You know, a dirty rotten scoundrel, so to speak.

Ah, quite a few hands. Some of you are looking around to see if your friends have their hands up. A few hands went up almost enthusiastically. Wonder what that means. Others are going up slowly and reluctantly. Maybe some of you just don't want to be accused of thinking you're perfect.

Some of your faces look confused, as though nobody ever explained sin before. Other faces have eyeballs practically rolling all over them like loose marbles — as though we said "bell-bottoms" or "Beastie Boys" or something else hopelessly out-dated.

Okay, let's try Stage Two. All you sinners who, *if you were left completely on your own,* would go straight to hell, raise your hands. Now I said *straight to hell* — do not pass "Go," do not collect two hundred dollars.

Wow! Not nearly so many hands this time, but lots of glares that say, "Look, guy, I'm not *that* bad!"

An Important Letter

I'm not sure I'd have the nerve to begin a talk that way. But then I'm not Paul — not by two thousand years and a few tons of sanctity. But it would be an excellent way to begin talking of one of Paul's most important letters, his Letter to the Romans.

Romans is different from Paul's other letters in two important ways. As far as we know, this is the only letter he wrote to Christians he had never met. All his others were to people to whom he had preached, people he wanted to stay in contact with. The Christians at Rome had heard the gospel from others. Paul was eager to meet them, however, and he had made definite plans to do so.

Meanwhile, the Romans had some pretty heavy questions that needed answers. In particular, questions about sin and about how to get out from under it. Paul wrote to answer those questions.

Since he had not met his audience, and since the topic was pretty heavy, Paul sounds more formal in Romans than in his other letters. In those you can almost imagine him dictating as he lounges around in an old pair of jeans. Romans, except for the final chapter, sounds like he's talking from a podium in a suit and tie.

But Romans isn't boring. As you walk through it, you'll find yourself at different times thinking things like "That was definitely not comforting. I really didn't care to hear that" or "Is he serious?" or "That's a lot better, thank God!"

This chapter can't give you a complete tour through Romans or anything close to that, but we can make a couple of major points and try to take some of the mystery out of the situation. Otherwise you may also find yourself thinking at times, "What is going on with these people?"

Speaking of Sin

One of the most important things Romans can do goes back to the start of this chapter. In the beginning of his letter, Paul describes a world without Christ — a world of people under the control of sin. Paul basically says, "The world is fouled up."

Two thousand years later we look around and agree with him. "Yeah, Paul, it's still pretty badly messed up."

At that point many of us tune out because we don't want to hear Paul's next point — namely, that we are *all* responsible. All of us! We are all sinners and the royal mess we call "today's society" has our own personal autograph on it too.

That's not a comforting thought. It's not something you roll through your mind over and over in order to feel great about yourself. And, incidentally, it's not the bottom line...but it is necessary. Otherwise you end up feeling you don't need Jesus. And when you feel you don't need Jesus, you're hurting without even knowing it.

But because our own sin is an uncomfortable idea, a common reaction goes like this: "Not me, man. I mean, not *really*. You don't see me planting terrorist bombs around innocent people, do you? Never robbed a bank or mugged a little old lady. I'm not a professional prostitute, a ruthless drug lord, a corrupt government official, or a bloodthirsty serial killer. I'm clean, man."

But how about the other day when you "borrowed" five bucks and yesterday when you put three pretty ugly bruises on your brother — or how about when you called your classmate a sexual ice cube because she doesn't get hot and heavy like you do or last weekend when...

"Oh, that! Hey, that's just ordinary stuff. Everybody does that. It's no big deal."

Who Needs Salvation?

"It's just ordinary stuff." As long as we can find somebody who's doing something worse, anything we do wrong is "no big deal."

No wonder we don't feel we need to be saved!

Let's pretend you fell off a cliff and were grasping onto a small tree growing out of the side a few feet below the edge. The tree begins to loosen. Below you are a couple thousand feet of nice pure air. After that, some really nasty rocks.

You're thinking of all the things that could have been but won't happen now. You're screaming, bawling, wishing you had another chance at life, wishing there was someone around. You'd settle for a three-year-old who could toddle off to get help. But you're all alone.

Suddenly out of nowhere someone leans down over the cliff and pulls you up. You'd definitely feel saved then!

It's a shame we can't all have an experience like that. It would give us an excellent — and realistic — way of thinking about sin, ourselves, and Jesus.

But most of us have never felt in immediate fatal danger, and certainly not because of our sins. Either we pretend they're not really sins or we relax and think back to what we've heard many times — "Jesus saved us" — as though the Jesus versus Sin match ended a long time ago — final score, Jesus one zillion, Sin zip. So we figure sin doesn't make any difference anymore. And then a really sneaky voice (guess where this comes from!) says, "So go ahead and sin. Hey, have some fun! It doesn't count anyway, remember?"

We Are All Sinners

In Romans, Paul writes about questions and problems much like those. First, he bluntly states, "Yeah, folks, like it or not we're all guilty. In different ways and for different reasons, perhaps, but one way or another we were all doomed — until Jesus."

Paul — and more importantly, God through Paul — is saying the same thing to us: "Jesus brings salvation — and you need it badly, baby."

And now a word for everyone who's thinking, "This kind of

35

religious talk sounds like a looney tune I heard being preached on a street corner. What about stuff that's nicer to hear — like how God is crazy in love with us because we're so wonderful in his sight? We can't be wonderful and sinners too."

Yes, we can — no problem.

Haven't you ever been furious with somebody you are also madly in love with — and maybe for good reason? When you were feeling furious, you probably didn't think about how much you love that person or remember any wonderful things about him or her.

In simple terms that's because we're little. We can only fit one or the other view into our minds and feelings at one time. But God is big. God doesn't have that limitation.

Are we wonderful and spectacular and amazing and lovable in God's sight? Yep.

Are we dirty rotten scoundrels doomed through our sins to a life without God? Yep.

Jesus came because both of those are true!

Jesus came to get us out of the mess we created — all of us together for the whole race and each of us individually for our own selves. That's why we call Jesus Savior, and that is Paul's theme in Romans.

Saved by Faith

How we receive that salvation, how it happens to us, is the big question that Paul addresses in Romans. It's still a hot topic among Christians today. You'll need more than this chapter to help sort it all out, but here's a basic background.

Some of Paul's audience, mostly the Jewish Christians, felt that salvation came from keeping the law that God had revealed to the Israelites. Today we'd say they had an attitude. "We're gonna make it because we know what's right and we've done it." In other words they felt they had engineered their own rescue from sin. One

Jewish practice in particular seemed to symbolize this: circumcision. That's why Paul refers to it so often.

To this attitude Paul says, "No way! Salvation from sin is incredibly big stuff. No puny human being can actually earn it, not even by keeping rules. And incidentally, which of you has actually kept all the rules? Uh-huh, that's what I thought."

So how does salvation come to us? Paul puts it in one word: *faith.* Faith in Jesus.

Now does that sound simple or what?

Actually, it is and then again it isn't. By faith Paul doesn't mean a simple little "Yeah, I believe in Jesus," after which we get back to our shopping or our video games. And he doesn't mean we can do whatever turns us on as long as we believe in Jesus. (See Romans 6:1-2 for Paul's no-nonsense answer to that idea.)

The faith that brings salvation is a faith that admits we've screwed up and can't make it on our own, but we believe that out of pure love Jesus bridged the huge distance our sins put between us and God. We're children of God again. And because that's what we are, *we will act like it!*

That's not an easy faith. It's not a little add-on faith like an extra button sewed onto a shirt in case we need it. It's not a cheap, empty faith that says, "I believe, man — now pass the bottle and let's raise some hell."

Stuff That Matters

Romans isn't easy, but don't let that stop you. There's something about the power of Paul's words in this Letter that draws you into what he's saying even when you're not completely clear on what he means. Maybe that's because our gut feeling instinctively tells us he's talking about stuff that really matters. When all the sitcoms and video games and weekend parties are over, what matters is where we stand with God.

CHAPTER FIVE

Sin City: The Rescue of Corinth

There it was in the distance — Sin City of the Empire. The place had quite a reputation! About six hundred thousand people lived there, and even if you considered yourself pretty street-smart, you probably would not have felt safe or comfortable around most of them.

From where the man stood, perhaps a mile or so away, he could almost hear the cursing, feel the fighting, smell the wine flowing, and see the men going away with the "women for rent."

The man was uneasy, even scared. He had felt that way before, but for different reasons. More than once he had been afraid for his life. But he had dodged the bullet (although there were no bullets then) several times, beginning with a nighttime escape in a large basket over the city walls of Damascus. (Kind of a first-century version of escape by hiding under the covers in the bed of a pickup truck.)

But this fear was different. It arose from a voice inside him that said, "This time it's not going to work, Paul. Not here, not in Corinth. There's too much going against you here."

An Unlikely Venture

The year was about 50 A.D. and Paul had good reason to think, "It's not going to work here." His job was to go into a place reeking with every type of moral crudity and tell the people to stop being foul and start believing in a crucified savior.

What kind of odds would Las Vegas give on a venture like that?

But Paul knew from experience that preaching the gospel had worked at times and in places where it didn't seem to stand a chance. The Lord had gotten him into some wild situations and had never let him down. So Paul entered Corinth, began his mission there, and stayed a year and a half — a very long time compared to other stopping points on his missionary journeys.

By the time he left, the unlikely had happened in spite of Paul's first fears (see 1 Corinthians 2:3). Brawling, lusting, drunken, foul-living Corinth now had a thriving group of Christians.

Paul's First Letter to Corinth

Because he had lived with them for quite some time, the Christians in Corinth held a special place in Paul's heart. He never saw them again as far as we know, but he kept in contact by letters. We have two of those letters, although we know there were others that did not survive.

When Paul wrote the Letter we now call First Corinthians, he was upset and concerned. The Corinthian Christians had lost it. Some were being rude and even cruel with one another, some had slipped back into crude practices, some were getting drunk even when they came together for worship, some were changing basic Christian beliefs, and some were gathering into snobbish cliques, claiming they were the *real Christians*.

Word about all of this got back to Paul — and I think I know how he felt (The comparison between Paul and me ends there.). The similarity I claim is that, about two millenniums apart, we both spend a good bit of time teaching about Jesus. I'm sure Paul has the edge on me, but I still know how he felt when he wrote that letter. It's what I feel when I see people like...I'll call him Terry.

Six years ago Terry was in my class. He was the kind of kid teachers point to and say, "There goes one of our best." He was into learning and sports and people and Jesus. He got a scholarship and a citizenship award — all without being stuck-up or weird.

Then came the weed and the bad dude friends and lots of other stuff. And, like Paul's Corinthians, Terry lost it!

That hurt. Not because I want to chalk up a great record for turning out young Christians but because I know Terry needs Jesus. I want Terry back into Jesus the way Paul wanted his Corinthians back into right living. Not to make Paul look good but to make sure they end up in a good place.

Words to Live By

Probably the single most practical thing you can say about the Bible is that it has a lot more to do with now than it does with then. Maybe the events happened a long time ago, and maybe we need to study a little about the world they happened in, but the meaning is for now.

And so, in many ways, we're all Corinthians. We all "lose it" from time to time. Maybe not in exactly the same ways they did. Maybe we don't lose it as badly as they did or maybe we're worse than they were. But our world, like the world of Corinth, doesn't exactly live and breathe and preach Jesus — and it rubs off on us.

Sometimes it happens little by little. One day we look around and realize we've become different. Or maybe someone like Paul has the guts to come up to us and tell us to get it back together. Reading First Corinthians can do that for us too. We just need to examine some of Paul's key themes.

Jesus and the World

Following Jesus doesn't make sense according to the way the world around us thinks. In First Corinthians you will find statements like "The message of the cross is complete absurdity to those who are headed for ruin, but to us who are experiencing salvation, it is the power of God."

Now Paul isn't telling us to deliberately make ourselves as weird as possible so people around us will say, "Wow, look at the geeks," and we can respond with, "Yeah, but we're gonna make it to heaven and you're gonna fry."

But he is reminding us that if we're Christian enough for it to actually show, the world may not rush out to give us a "Totally Cool Award." Much of the world goes by different standards than the ones Jesus gave us. We're not always going to fit in.

Also, Jesus chose to remain with us in a spectacular way through the Eucharist, and we need to keep in mind what that really is. In Chapter Eleven some of the Corinthians had apparently forgotten the meaning of the Eucharist. According to Paul's description of their behavior, it seems as though they came to the liturgies more to snip at one another and party than to celebrate the presence and love of Jesus among them.

This passage provides us with a good opportunity to run a check on how much we appreciate the Mass, and especially the Eucharist. Okay, some of the hymns don't exactly hit the top of the musical excitement scale. Like you, I've attended some liturgies that seemed like they were planned to be boring as a deliberate test of my faith.

But even if that happens, we need to remember what's really going on beneath the ordinary-looking wrapper — we are contacting Jesus more closely than if he were standing right next to us in church, giving us a hug.

Paul was firm in reminding the Corinthians that receiving Jesus in the Eucharist was not an ordinary action that could be done without thought. Sometimes we all need that same reminder.

The Love Connection

Another key theme from First Corinthians is that we're all in this together. You're familiar with the story of Paul's conversion on the road to Damascus — the blinding light and the voice of Jesus saying, "Why are you persecuting me?" (Acts 9:4).

Notice that Jesus didn't ask Paul why he was persecuting his followers. He said me. And when Paul asked who was speaking, the Lord answered, "I am Jesus, whom you are persecuting" (Acts 9:5).

Paul's famous description of us as the Body of Christ might have its roots in this first experience of Jesus. In Chapter Twelve he explains: "As a body is one though it has many parts, and all the parts of the body, though many, are one body, so also Christ" (1 Corinthians 12:12). And later, "Now you are Christ's body, and individually parts of it" (1 Corinthians 12:27).

We are all invisibly connected. A fantastic spiritual network joins us. In the next world the invisibility will be lifted and we'll get to see how it all operates. But for now we can help good things to happen to one another by our relationships and our prayers. Unfortunately, we can cause bad things to happen to one another when we mess up. It's not just ourselves who are getting hurt.

Love — the Real Version

Next to the Sermon on the Mount, First Corinthians (13:4-7) contains the best-known passage from the New Testament. Except for genuine Satanists, everybody loves love — and we usually like to think of ourselves as loving persons.

So we're glad to hear Paul say that love is what counts. When it comes to God's bottom line, you don't have to be smart or powerful, as long as you're loving.

In fact, Paul says that if you're smart or powerful or even *religious* but you're not living your life with love, none of the rest has any value at all.

So love as the biggie sounds pretty good — and it is. But we need to make sure we've got the right understanding of love.

Paul's famous description shows us how challenging true love is. If the world's version of love ("You light my fire...this feels so right.") starts to seem like the real thing, keep going back to First Corinthians.

Find the Right Words

Some sections of First Corinthians are Paul's responses to questions about problems of that particular time, based on that culture, and they no doubt sound a little silly today. One example is Paul's insistence that women let their hair grow — but keep their heads covered! We would need a scholar and a good bit of space to explain the customs and culture that prompted Paul to make such statements — as well as the religious principle he had in mind.

When you come to a section like that, put it on hold and don't let it distract you from the sections that can help you realize all over again the life you have been called to live.

CHAPTER SIX

Telling It Like It Is: Paul's "Get Tough" Letter

Outside our parish church, Paul is a hunk of stone. He stands to the right of the steps leading to the front door. Paul the apostle, the great missionary preacher...carved in stone. He looks out at the traffic and watches the guys who sneak out for a smoke when the homily is dull.

The "Unreal" Paul

I'm glad Paul is there in stone today, but it's a shame we too often think of him as having been made of stone when he was alive, or as a robot who came along at the right time to act out the following early Christian script.

First Paul persecuted Christians like death itself. Then God knocked some sense into his head on the road to Damascus. After that he went around preaching like crazy, floating from one place to another on a nonstop Jesus high, feeling only the joy of being in the Christianity business. When Paul spoke, people listened, believed, got baptized, and lived as model Christians.

But that's not how it was — and that's not a picture of the real Paul.

The real Paul was a saint all right. But not because he floated around on a Christian cloud, not because he zapped his listeners with such Christian energy that they lived happily ever after in Jesus land, and not because he was made of saintly concrete and never felt anything but a holy high.

Second Corinthians will cure unrealistic, sugar-sweet ideas like those in a hurry. Read it. You'll get a glimpse into the personal Paul that you won't come close to anywhere else.

Life in Sin City

Here's the background. The Corinthian Christians were special to Paul because he had lived among them for a year and a half. They were such an unlikely group of converts to the Christian life, living in the Sin City of the Roman Empire, and he was proud of them.

A few years after he left Corinth, major problems and questions arose in the community. Paul wrote the letter we call First Corinthians in response to those problems. That seemed to help for a while, and Paul may have visited the Corinthians briefly sometime later — but we're not sure.

Then came more trouble, and some of it aimed very personally at Paul. He was being bad-mouthed both by people in the original community and by some new arrivals spouting new and wrong teachings. That hurt Paul in two ways: he felt personally betrayed, and he knew that his Corinthian Christians were being led away from the truth.

So he wrote a letter that didn't get preserved. Paul refers to it several times in Second Corinthians. It's often called the "severe letter." Apparently, it wasn't exactly full of warm hugs and kisses by mail. He sent the letter by way of his coworker Titus, wondering whether it would totally turn his Corinthians off or restore their friendship.

As it turned out, Titus' and Paul's "severe letter" seemed to straighten things out fairly well for a while. Later Paul wrote to the Christians in Corinth still another time — the letter we call Second Corinthians today. Things were a little better, it seems, but they still were not completely okay.

Ministry of Reconciliation

What does Paul want of this relationship with his Corinthians? He tells them in Chapters Five and Six. He wants them to accept the "ministry of reconciliation" that he came to preach.

Basically this ministry says, "We screwed up — it's called sin. We would have been dead meat, but God didn't give up on us. He sent Jesus. Please believe that and act on it. We've got another chance, and it can be so terrific. So please don't blow it!"

Then Paul includes a personal note (6:3-13) that in today's words might go like this: "I've done my best to get this across to you, and I've put up with a lot of crud to do it, all because I really care. So please don't turn off what I'm saying." Paul hopes his words won't turn them off to the gospel message. He almost begs for acceptance. As you read the verses, you can feel Paul's pain.

That happens today too. And it's because God chose to let us in on his act.

In many ways it would be a lot smoother if God took each of us aside, privately and individually, maybe even transported us to another planet to do this, where he would explain the whole story, one-on-one. He would outline what he wants us to believe and do. Then he would challenge us: "Buy it or don't buy it. Choose for me or against me."

Instead God decided to teach and challenge us through other people, and that creates difficulties we wouldn't have going one-on-one with God.

Teachers Who Care

People who preach and teach the Christian faith are convinced of what they know and say. Obviously, they want others to accept it too.

Sure, a few may be on a power trip. ("I made Christians out of thirty-seven people last month, and they all believe exactly the same things I do. That's better than the national evangelical average.") But that doesn't describe most teachers and preachers of the gospel.

Most of them just want good things for the people they're talking to and care about. The more strongly they believe and the more they love the people they're talking to, the more they want those people to accept the gospel.

But these teachers of the Faith are not perfect. Sometimes they don't communicate well. Sometimes they misjudge. Sometimes, like the rest of us, they just plain do or say wrong things.

On top of that, the people who listen are free human beings. They have the right to a free choice. Otherwise, accepting faith wouldn't mean anything. People are free to decide that this whole gospel/church stuff is pretty much nonsense.

But if they do decide this, that doesn't mean it *is* nonsense. The decisions of individuals don't change reality. For example, you are free to decide that this is the year 1787 if you want to, but that doesn't *make* it 1787. It's still this year, this month, this day.

Kind of a messy situation, isn't it? That's where Paul found himself when he wrote to his Corinthians. And it's where we all find ourselves whenever we try to share our faith or whenever we listen to others sharing their faith with us.

In a way Chapter Four, verse seven, puts this whole situation into a terrific little summary. It's even been made into a hymn you might recognize — we possess this treasure (God's message, God's truth, God's love) "in earthen vessels."

Faith in Action

"We pause now for these messages." That means a commercial is coming, right? You've known this since the days when you rode a tricycle.

In a way that happens in Second Corinthians too. All of a sudden, in Chapters Eight and Nine, Paul talks about "the collection," and he makes it pretty clear that he hopes the Corinthians will give generously to it. This is a big change of pace from the first part of the letter, and it needs some explanation.

The Christians in Jerusalem were going through tough times. Tough doesn't mean they couldn't cover the price of Matthew-Levi 801 jeans at the Jerusalem East Mall. Tough means they were really hurting.

Paul tried to do something about this. He challenged people in cities where he preached to put their faith into action by helping others. He established a fund, a collection, for the relief of the poor in Jerusalem. In these two chapters he tries to persuade the Corinthians to come across with some bucks for the cause.

This section is so different that some people thought it was originally from a different letter. But in a way it was not that drastic a switch. Paul is hoping the Corinthians will act like Christians. So what's that got to do with giving money?

Actually, quite a bit.

Okay, religion and money haven't always been a good mix. From the beginnings of Christianity down through the television age, some people have used religion to make money for themselves. ("For a twenty-five-dollar love offering to help this ministry, we will send you absolutely free this beautiful hardbound book entitled….") Others have tried to use their money to buy God. ("I know what I do ain't always the way God would want it, Father, but maybe this check for fifty grand to help build the orphanage….")

Finally, we've heard it's easier to give money than to give

yourself — your time, your attention, your genuine caring. Parents who buy their kids things but seldom share themselves are a good example of this.

No Easy Way Out

All true enough. But I don't think giving money is always such an easy way out. That might have been true a few decades ago when a teenager was rich if he or she owned a radio, a record player, and a stack of forty-fives. These days money is harder to part with. The clothing and entertainment industries in particular work overtime making exciting new products.

So parting with some of your portion of the several billion dollars that American teenagers spend every year is a challenge. But try taking up that challenge now and then. Money is not a substitute for prayer and relationship with God, and money is no substitute for love — but sometimes it can be a sign of it.

It's really awfully easy to say a quick Our Father, Hail Mary, and Glory Be for the starving people in Ethiopia and then take off for the mall to drop twenty bucks on a couple of new tapes. ("Okay, God, the ball's in your court now. You take care of Ethiopia.")

Try putting the twenty in the mail instead of taking it to the mall (or half of it anyway). See if you don't feel pretty good. For some motivation from Saint Paul, check out Second Corinthians 9:7.

Paul's Pain

And now we switch you to still another track. This section (Chapters Ten through Twelve) is Paul's explosion of frustration. Again, its tone is so different that some scholars have thought it was originally part of another letter of Paul's.

But Paul didn't write his letters all at once, sitting at a typewriter. Writing was a slow process back then. When he wrote this section, he could have been in a drastically different mood, and he also may have received some additional news in the meantime.

The situation is that some people have been bad-mouthing Paul in Corinth again, trying to ruin his legitimate authority and leadership of the Corinthian Christians. Paul sarcastically calls these slanderers the "super apostles."

Paul feels pain and anger. He's not like a strong-armed general, furious over the disobedience of some of his troops. He's more like a father, deeply hurt and upset that some of his children would doubt him and turn away from him.

So he explodes. He doesn't talk very sweetly. He attacks. He gets sarcastic. He boasts of what he's done and gone through.

That may seem strange behavior for someone whose job is to preach love and the Prince of Peace.

Telling It Like It Is

Paul makes it very clear that he doesn't get a charge out of writing and behaving this way, that it's not his style. He also makes it clear why he's doing it anyway.

It's not to pin hero medals on himself. Paul is convinced he has the truth, God's revealed truth, the *real stuff*. He loves his Corinthian "children" and can't stand to see them being led astray. He wants to bring them back. If that means getting tough and talking rough to reassert himself in their eyes, Paul can handle it.

No emotionless concrete Paul here. This is Paul with his hands curled into fists and a razor edge in his voice. Notice that he doesn't wish evil to his adversaries, nor does he say they're going to fry in hell. But he does take a vehement stand.

If we remember the "earthen vessels," Paul's behavior isn't so strange at all. It would be nice if the kingdom of God could be spread always and only by means of tender words, affectionate hugs, and warm peaceful relationships among everyone — but that's not always possible.

Sometimes we have to get tough and tell things the way they really are, even though it's painful for everybody at the time. It's just going to be that way sometimes. Second Corinthians gives us an example from the very beginnings of our faith.

CHAPTER SEVEN

Four Small New Testament Jewels

There was this guy who loved baseball so much he couldn't imagine life without it. He wondered if there would be baseball in the next life, so he prayed and prayed to find out. Finally, an angel brought him an answer.

"I've got good news and bad news," the angel said. "The good news is — there is baseball in the next life."

"Wonderful. What's the bad news?"

"You're pitching tonight."

For most of us, that second part *would* be bad news. If an angel asked us if we wanted to go to heaven, we'd answer "Sure!" Who doesn't? But if the angel continues, "How about now?" — well, that's a bit different.

"Now? Are you *crazy*? No way!"

That's how I'd probably respond. Sure, I want to go to heaven. But part of me wants to get in a few more games of racquetball first, just in case heaven doesn't have a court. Chances are you wouldn't jump at the chance to walk through the heavenly gates right this minute either.

That shows we've got a long way to go before we reach the attitude Paul had when he wrote his Letter to the Philippians.

We're going to look at Philippians, Colossians, and First and Second Thessalonians. It'll be a bit like touring England, Scotland, Ireland, and Wales all in one day. Compared to some other countries, they're relatively small. But they're full of great things to see.

Compared to Paul's other letters, these four are relatively small, but they are packed full of some of the greatest things he ever wrote. We'll pick out some major themes.

The Final Score

1. *This life isn't all of it!* Whether you are soaring or sinking (by this world's standards), whether your life feels like an amusement park or a concentration camp, this isn't the final score.

Paul wrote to the Philippians from prison, where he was uncertain of his future. Would he be let out? Brought to trial, condemned, and executed? Left to rot in prison for years?

Paul didn't know. Paul didn't care, either.

That fact comes across clearly in Philippians 1:12-26. If he dies soon, that's fine. In fact, he leans toward that preference. But if not, that's okay too. He can see some advantages in hanging around the planet a bit longer.

You might say that when it came to life or death, Paul was pretty easy to please.

Not that being in prison turned him into an early Christian loony tune. He simply saw things as they are so clearly that he lived them and felt them.

These are the same things we know. We know them and even say them out loud when someone like a religion teacher asks for the "right" answer. The things of this life aren't the really important things. What really counts is living for Jesus and spending forever in heaven with him and the Father and the Holy Spirit.

We *say* that — and then go out and have a major cow over

something like our pizza not having enough pepperoni on it or missing our favorite airhead sitcom to study for a math test.

Prisons aren't very nice places today, and in Paul's time they must have been worse. In spite of that, Paul told the Philippians to rejoice! He says it with such great feeling that we can tell he himself is rejoicing.

This wasn't an empty, dizzy, "don't worry, be happy" routine that fakes happiness by simply tuning out problems. Ignoring problems wasn't Paul's style. When his reputation and authority were attacked, he defended himself passionately. And one of his biggest concerns was the success of a collection for the poor of Jerusalem.

The joy Paul recommends comes from knowing that no matter what kind of crud is trying to spoil your day, it's temporary. You have what counts — Jesus and his promise of eternal life.

When Jesus Comes Again

2. *The Second Coming of Jesus.* On this item there are very few "in-between" Christians. Mention the Second Coming to a random group of one hundred Christians, and you'll probably get instant attention from forty-nine and a blank look or a big yawn from another forty-nine.

Nearly all Christians believe Jesus will come again, somehow, sometime. After all, he clearly said he would. What isn't clear is the when and the how. To individual Christians that's either a big issue or it's not.

In Paul's time it was a *Very Big Issue,* particularly among the Thessalonians. Many thought Jesus would return soon to reclaim his faithful followers and bring them to heaven. This was causing some problems.

One problem was that some Thessalonian Christians were worried sick about loved ones who had died. What a rip it would be, they felt, if those people didn't make it to heaven just because old age or a really nasty germ got to them before Jesus did.

A second problem was that some saw the Second Coming as a reason to take life *very* easy. For example, in our time someone who thinks the end of the world will happen next week might go wild with charge cards and have a ball. Something like that was happening among certain Thessalonian Christians. They were becoming professional loafers.

So Paul told them not to be so hyper about the Second Coming. God will never let a little thing like death keep his loved ones from him. Jesus conquered sin and death — that's what faith in him is all about! When he comes again, he'll gather all his followers from all ages of history.

As for exactly when this will happen...well, just get back to work, guys and gals!

Hidden Truths

Two thousand years later we're still pretty much in the dark about the Second Coming. We believe it's going to happen, but the when and the how are still hidden.

Some Christians seem to have it fairly well figured out. They base their certainty on their interpretation of 1 Thessalonians 4:16-17, on parts of the letters of John, and on Jesus' own words in Matthew 24:29-42.

You may have heard this description of the last days yourself: As the result of great disbelief and evil caused by a powerful enemy of Jesus, the earth will suffer huge global destruction for a while, but Jesus will literally come down to the planet, riding a cloud of glory, to snatch his followers up to heaven with him. These items are often called the Antichrist, the Tribulation, and the Rapture.

Could that happen? Of course it could. God is in charge and can do whatever seems like a good idea to him. But the Scripture verses involved here use what's called *apocalyptic* language. In the simplest possible terms, this means we have to be very careful about taking it literally.

The best advice is what Jesus himself gave in Matthew 25:13 and which Paul echoes in 1 Thessalonians 5:6: Be prepared for the end, whether that means your own death or the end of the world.

In either case, as long as you're prepared to meet the Lord, it's a good deal. This was Paul's attitude, remember. If death comes next Tuesday, look at all the research papers and final exams you won't have to do. If it's not for quite a while, you'll have to do those final exams, but think of all the parties you can go to afterward.

Treasury of Beliefs

3. *Some heavy stuff about Jesus.* Even if the Second Coming is a million years away, Christians will still be working on the mystery when it happens. Mystery doesn't mean we know almost nothing; it simply means that with our limited human intelligence, we'll never have it completely figured out.

But Paul gave us a lot to go on in sections of Philippians and Colossians (Philippians 2:5-11 and Colossians 1:15-20). Originally those sections were probably short hymns sung by the early Christians. Paul quoted them and expanded upon them.

Spend some time on Philippians 2:5-11. A treasury of our beliefs about Jesus is contained there in capsule form. Here are some of them. Jesus was really and fully God and really and fully human; he didn't just look like a human being — he *was* one. When he became a human being, he kept on being God, even though he had to learn like any other true human being.

We sometimes use words from philosophy to say these things more clearly, phrases like "one person with two natures — human and divine." That's fine because we need technical terms to make sure we have the ideas straight. But these terms tend to make Jesus as appealing as a cracker that's been lying on the kitchen counter for days.

Actually, the consequences of Jesus being both fully divine and fully human are beautifully wild and breathtaking. Any and every human action except sin is now a channel between us and God. God can communicate to us through it.

Got a headache? Feel discouraged? Did something terrific happen that makes you feel positively and naturally high? Do you feel the glow of friendship? Feel hungry? Feel warmly well-fed after a good meal? Feel dead tired or full of energy? Do you appreciate a great sunrise? Do you like moonlit nights?

These are no longer just human feelings because Jesus has been there. We can learn about God in and from all of them — and we can offer them back to God.

"Great sunshine, great breeze, Lord. Excellent pizza too."

"Thanks. Glad you noticed."

Jesus Needs No Additions

4. *One savior is all we need — and all there is.* Every now and then, Christians try to improve on Christ. They add something to try to make the salvation Jesus earned for us "work better," so to speak. Often they mean well when they do so, but these so-called improvements can be dangerous. We don't need them. All we need is Jesus.

Here is one example of a well-meaning but excessive "addition" to Scripture. Jesus saved us from our sins, yes — but what really counts is knowing how the drought of 1988 (along with every other major event) was foretold in the Book of Revelation!

Another example: Jesus opened the gates of heaven, yes — but if you want to really make sure you'll get there, say this special prayer nineteen times on the third Tuesday of every month except February of leap year. Then you'll have salvation locked up and on ice.

Another example: Jesus was a great savior, yes — but he's just one manifestation of God on earth. Buddha and Muhammad and a bunch of other people did and taught the same things in different ways.

Another example: Jesus is God's Word to us, sure, and it's good to read the Bible — but in the Bible, what led the wise men to Jesus? A star! So right there God is telling us to consult the stars to get his real message. Astrology and Christianity are practically the same thing! Jesus himself was a Capricorn, and that explains why he…

This sort of absurdity has been going on since Paul's time, so in Colossians Paul warns about it. A small capsule can be found in Chapter Two, verse eight.

Now it's important to understand what we're *not* saying here. We're not saying that all faiths except the Christian faith have everything completely fouled up or that we can learn nothing from them. We're not saying that every kind of human knowledge, like psychology, is worthless because it has nothing to do with God. As a matter of fact, we share and have learned valuable things from other faith traditions, and sciences like psychology help us understand ourselves, which helps us understand how we relate to God.

It's just that nothing can take the place of Jesus.

Small Jewels

We've only skimmed the surface of Philippians, Colossians, and First and Second Thessalonians. There's much, much more in these small jewels from the New Testament. Spend some time with them.

And, by the way, one of the few things they don't talk about is whether or not there is baseball in heaven.

CHAPTER EIGHT

A Truly Gothic Glance at Hebrews

Have you ever done one of those thought-starting activities where you compare yourself to some type of car or flower or animal? "If I were an animal, I'd be a _____," and then you fill in an animal and describe the similarities between yourself and an eagle or a chipmunk or a baboon.

Psychologists and creative-writing teachers use this technique a lot. It works well if the respondents know the results will be read only by someone they trust. But if the comparison is going to be (gasp!) "shared with the group" and the category is cars, ninety-five percent of the population will call themselves Cadillacs or Porsches or Lamborghinis. I've tried this in creative-writing class, and nobody has yet compared himself or herself to a '72 Dodge station wagon or a '53 Chevy pickup.

The Many Places of God

I like to use this activity with Scripture, comparing New Testament letters to different styles of churches. For example, the First Letter of John would be a small cozy chapel with warm wood tones, carpeting, comfortable pews, interesting little niches and shrines, and lots of friendly flickering candles, the kind of church where you can almost feel God hugging you.

Romans would be an impressive formal-looking church with very straight precise lines — the kind that gets you thinking about what's real and right in life and what's not.

And then there's Hebrews. Hebrews would be a huge Gothic cathedral with massive columns and pillars reaching to a ceiling so high you can barely see it. The sanctuary and altar are off in the distance; everything is made of marble and gold, and the air is faintly sweet with the scent of candle wax and incense. It's the kind of church where you whisper because you are aware of the awesomeness of God.

It's good that we have different styles of churches with different atmospheres. We learn something equally true and valid about God in each of them. And it's good that each of the New Testament letters has its own atmosphere and scope.

But with Hebrews, that gives us a problem. Throughout this booklet I've often said, "This chapter will only touch the surface." Well, with Hebrews, we won't even be able to touch all of the surface.

That Old-time Religion

Who wrote the Letter to the Hebrews? We really don't know. Possibly it was a disciple of Saint Paul. But if we believe that Hebrews is an inspired writing, part of God's written message to us, it really doesn't matter who wrote it.

What is important is the original audience, the people for whom Hebrews was written. They were almost certainly Jewish Christians, people who had been raised in the Jewish faith, the faith of the Old Testament, and who had embraced faith in Jesus.

The Hebrew Christians believed that Jesus had fulfilled the promise of a messiah, but they had questions about how the faith they grew up with related to Jesus. What about the "old" religious practices and rituals? Did they count for anything? Should they keep on practicing them? It's a pretty fair guess that most of them missed some of those old ceremonies.

For this reason Hebrews, probably more than any other New Testament writings, requires some knowledge of the Old Testament in order to understand many parts of it. Please don't let that scare you away. You don't need a graduate degree in Scripture to wrap your mind around a single verse.

You can read Hebrews for parts that make sense to you. When you come across a section that seems to have come from the ceiling of that Gothic cathedral, don't say "This is seriously far out" and close the pages for good. Just begin with a few basic concepts.

God and Us

Sometimes we act and think as though all we need is to throw a little mental switch, send a "you're cool" thought toward heaven, and that takes care of everything that needs to happen between God and us. One of the key ideas in Hebrews is that the relationship between God and his people is more than just flicking some simple mental switch.

We should all know this, of course, because relationships don't work that easily in other areas of our life. A guy doesn't just send a nice thought to his girlfriend on her birthday. Not if he's serious about the relationship. Husbands and wives don't just say "Have a nice day" to each other on their anniversary and let it drop. If we've hurt a loved one deeply, just saying "I'm sorry" isn't going to repair the relationship. Thoughts and words are important, but they have to be fleshed out by actions and events. That's how life is. Relationships demand action.

So when the relationship between God and his people got messed up because of sin, it took more than flicking a little mental switch ("Sorry, God!") to fix it. Which brings us to the idea of sacrifice, a central concept in Hebrews.

The Perfect Sacrifice

Sacrifice is an ancient idea. It is an element of nearly every religion. In a ceremony of sacrifice, a person, usually called a priest, brings something material to a place that represents the god of that religion. The offering is changed at the altar in a way that takes it out of ordinary life, ordinary use, to show that it is now part of their god's sacred dimension.

Just as in these other religions, our offerings demonstrate our desire to belong to God ourselves. In simple terms, it says, "We don't want to belong to this world, we don't want to belong to sin anymore, we want to belong to you."

Because of sin, we needed to do this — we needed to re-belong to God — and God showed us how to do this. In fact, he did it for us, but he started gradually and worked slowly.

When God first began to teach us in Old Testament times, he taught us, through the Israelites, to use animal sacrifices. He didn't want his people using the human sacrifices that their pagan neighbors used.

There were many different sacrifices in Israelite rituals, but the key sacrifice ("We want to belong back to you, we want to make up for our sins.") happened once a year. On that day the high priest alone entered the most sacred part of the Temple, the inner sanctuary, or "holy of holies." There he poured the blood of the sacrificed animal on the altar, which represented God.

But God is BIG, and therefore so is his relationship with his people, and so was the damage that sin had done to that relationship. Animal sacrifices just didn't cut it in repairing the damage.

So God sent Jesus, who was both God and a perfect human being — the perfect sacrifice. Jesus was also the perfect high priest making the offering, representing us in both roles. The author of Hebrews is trying very hard to explain that Jesus is *it,* the ultimate — the one who, in extremely plain terms, got the job done. In so doing, the author makes references you may not completely understand.

Jesus Had to Be!

Hebrews doesn't say that the Old Testament rituals were worthless. In much the same way that Paul discusses circumcision, the author of Hebrews says that these rituals were valuable as a *sign* of what was to come, a preparation. But they weren't it — Jesus is.

> Just as it is appointed that human beings die once, and after this the judgment, so also Christ, offered once to take away the sins of many, will appear a second time, not to take away sin but to bring salvation to those who eagerly await him.
> (Hebrews 9:27-28)

Most of us don't need to be convinced that the ritual sacrifices of Israelite times no longer need to be repeated. And we probably don't need to be convinced that Jesus is superior to the angels, which is the topic of the first two chapters. But that doesn't mean we're not a good audience for the messages in Hebrews.

One of the great things we can gain from reading Hebrews is a new sense of who Jesus was and what he did. His life, death, and rising aren't just an inspirational story from which we can learn to talk nicely to people, help little brothers and sisters with homework, not hog the pizza, and stay away from the local joint dealer.

Those are all good to do or good to avoid, but Jesus is far more than the best-ever example of being nice and living a straight life. Sin had created a cosmic distance between God and people, a gap that couldn't be fixed by flicking a mental switch. Something had to *happen,* an offering had to be made to repair the damage and bridge the distance.

God Is God

You may prefer the cozy little chapel to the great Gothic cathedral. It is more comfortable to think of God wrapping his arms around us in a big hug than to think of him as an awesome presence completely different from us. So Hebrews is not some people's favorite New Testament letter.

It seems to present God as rather distant, in spite of the fact that sin's damage has been repaired. It even has some awfully stern verses, such as "It is a fearful thing to fall into the hands of the living God" (Hebrews 10:31). This verse refers to someone who has known and accepted the truth of faith and then knowingly and deliberately throws it out.

It's always a good idea to listen to all sides of a story, even though they sometimes say opposite things. That's especially true in the case of our relationship with God. But in his case even the things that seem to be opposite, or at least very different, are equally true at the same time. Why? Because God is God, and he will never fit into our relatively tiny brain capacity.

Is God as close to us as our own blood and breath? Does God say, "I will remember your sins no more," and wrap us in a huge loving, forgiving embrace? Yes.

Is God mighty, majestic, and awesome? Is he incredibly different and *other* than us? Determined to crush and wipe out every trace of evil wherever it is found? Yes.

Both are true at the same time.

God is always God!

Headed for Glory

Even though Hebrews seems to feature more of the second aspect of God, it's a comforting letter in many ways. "Since through the blood of Jesus we have confidence of entrance into the sanctuary...let us approach with a sincere heart and in absolute trust" (Hebrews 10:19, 22).

In particular, Hebrews stresses that Jesus was one of us. Although he didn't sin, he was no stranger to the attraction of evil. He went through all the pain and stress of life that we do — in fact, more so. He knows what it's like to be a human being on planet Earth. That should give us confidence.

> For we do not have a high priest who is unable to sympathize with our weaknesses, but one who has similarly been tested in every way, yet without sin. So let us confidently approach the throne of grace to receive mercy and to find grace for timely help.
>
> (Hebrews 4:15-16)

In the 1950s a Catholic bishop named Fulton Sheen had a live national television show. One Tuesday evening he talked about the humanity of Jesus and closed with the statement, "We have a God who *stumbled* to his throne!"

We stumble a lot too. But if we keep the Faith, we're headed toward a throne of glory. And along the way, even when we're kneeling in the huge spaciousness of that great Gothic cathedral, God is very near.

CHAPTER NINE

Revelation: Who Needs It?

One of the kids mentioned below needs to read the Book of Revelation, that strange and wonderful book of the New Testament full of cosmic battles and wild symbols. Everyone can benefit from Revelation's message, of course, but one of the following kids *really* needs it. Which one?

Who Needs It?

Craig read an article in the *National Confuser* about an ancient manuscript that supposedly describes silver-skinned visitors driving great chariots through the sky. The visitors threatened to return and scatter everything apart if earthlings "try to reach the sky in chariots of their own."

The paper quotes a "top scientist and Bible expert" who says that the story is amazingly similar to the Tower of Babel story in Chapter Eleven of Genesis. This expert says it could mean God considers our technology sinful and is planning to use a race of superior beings to put an end to the earth as we know it. This bothers Craig, and he wants to know what the Bible says about the end of the world.

Colleen is lying across her bed sobbing. For two years she's been in a small group of close friends. Lately, several have been living a little on the wild side, but things have never gotten too heavy, so Colleen has stayed with the group.

But tonight Tracey, one of the group, has engineered that activity known as a party with no parents around. All the other girls are going. Tracey has invited "guys who really know how to party," and they're bringing "real party" supplies.

Four days ago Colleen told Tracey she wouldn't be there. Moreover, she made the mistake of saying she thinks the party is wrong and could get out of hand. In other words, she had the guts to give a Christian response to the situation.

Since then life has been a moderate hell for her. Her locker at school gets decorated with signs like "Miss Priss" and "Miss Straight." (Those are two of the nicer signs.) She finds notes like "If you are a narc, you die." Except for insults and name-calling, her former friends don't speak to her.

It's getting to be a lot for Colleen to handle. She's wondering if it would be so bad to show up at the party — as long as she didn't let things get out of control. She could have a couple of drinks so her friends would think she's cool. What would be wrong with that? If a guy throws some hormones in her direction, she could respond enough to show she's normal, but not too much.

That's beginning to look like a better idea than staying home tonight and facing more ugliness on Monday.

What Price Faith?

Who most needs the message of Revelation? Not Craig. He needs something to calm his anxiety about how the world will end, but he won't find that in Revelation.

It's Colleen who needs the message. Her situation is a twentieth-century teenage parallel of the situation the original readers of

Revelation were in. Her circumstances aren't quite as heavy, but there are similarities.

Those early Christians, Revelation's original audience, were being hassled for their faith — and they were paying for it in major ways. Sometimes the price was death.

From a nonfaith point of view, it looked as though the Roman Empire was the ultimate force in the world. It looked as though Nero and the emperors who followed him were *really* in charge, the baddest of the really cool bad dudes who swagger around and seem to have power to say who's okay and who's not. (Nero, incidentally, is the villain referred to in that famous 666.) So it was easy for Christians in those times to wonder about their faith and ask, "Is this really worth it?"

It was even more tempting to wonder if giving in to the raunchy, sinful culture would be so bad after all. "Just a little here, a little there…what's the harm? After all, we believe in Jesus. He already saved us. What's the problem with making our lives a little easier?" In other words, having it both ways: counting on being saved by Jesus and deliberately going along with and enjoying the very sins Jesus saved us from. It's the ultimate "have your cake and eat it too" package.

The Winning Team

That's the situation Revelation was written in, and it's not exactly mysterious. In fact, it probably sounds extremely familiar. What makes Revelation seem so far out is the apocalyptic writing style the author chose. In a nutshell, apocalyptic writing uses vivid symbols and what seems like a vision of the future *principally to get across a message about the present.*

Although the structure and symbolism in Revelation may be complicated, the message isn't. The message is extremely simple, up-front, even positively blunt. It was clear to the original readers who were familiar and comfortable with apocalyptic writing.

Basically, it's this: *Jesus won!* The battle is already decided! (That's the part that "tells the future.") Right now times are tough, but don't give up or give in — because if we hang in with Jesus, we win too! (That's the "message for the present.")

Revelation is a Christian pep talk, a spiritual psych-up. One part offers encouragement and reassurance: "Because of Jesus, you're on the winning side!" The other offers a warning and a challenge: "So don't blow it by deliberately sneaking over to the other side now and then!"

Social Suicide?

In our opening example, Colleen isn't facing execution, but at her age social death can seem even worse. Going along with what's wrong in order to avoid it is awfully tempting. She needs the message of Revelation.

So do the rest of us — all who want to be Christian but....There are a lot of us like that.

I want to be a Christian, absolutely, no doubt, for sure — but...well, later. Hand me a Bible along with my wheelchair and I'll sit there and be a red-hot senior Christian the rest of my life.

I want to be a Christian, yes, indeed, sign me up — but not this weekend. There's a real party on this weekend.

I want to be a Christian — but not this Sunday morning. I gotta catch up on sleep. Maybe next week.

I want to be a Christian — but only if it gives me a spiritual rush and makes me feel terrific. After all, you gotta feel something to get into it.

Strength vs. Wimpiness

Revelation makes it clear that the Christian life has no room for deliberate wimpiness like that. And we need to get straight about strength vs. wimpiness.

It sometimes looks as though the hell-raisers of the world are the strong ones. They try to give themselves that image and probably end up believing it. They talk about Christians in terms of weakness.

"No guts," they tell you when you turn down a drink you shouldn't have. "No guts," they say to people who won't go along with them to rip off a stereo or a VCR. "No (whatever)," they say to classmates who won't get on the local "sexually active" list. They paint Christians as dumb, as suckers and losers, for putting their loyalty into faith in another world.

Unfortunately, some Christians start buying that. They wonder if they really are suckers and if maybe the cool-acting hell-raisers and rule-breakers are the winners in "real life" because they know how to have "real fun."

And all the time it's the other way around, totally the other way around. Following every little urge — right or wrong, no matter what it is, you gotta have it — that's weak!

As for winners and losers, we already know who they are. It's all wrapped up, and there isn't even a one-centimeter question mark about it. Because of the difference between time and eternity, the game is still going on here on earth. But the final score is already on the record books. Jesus won! Complete wipeout! What's being played here on earth is people choosing whose side they want to be on.

It sometimes looks like the other side has more power and/or more fun, making that the smart side to be on. But that's pure raw you-know-what. Don't put it on your plate and swallow it because later on it has a real bad taste.

Good Guys and Bad Guys

Revelation is very up-front in talking about opposing sides, good guys and bad guys. But we have a problem with it, and there are good reasons for our problem.

At one time — not very long ago — Christians talked and thought in terms of good guys and bad guys very easily. Christians were good guys; hell-raisers and general nonbelievers were bad guys. Simple. Way too simple.

Christians who think that way start acting in ways that aren't very Christian. It's easy to get conceited, like the Pharisee who thanked God that he was so much better than other people. It's easy to begin giving yourself the credit for being saved, as though you have yourself to thank, not Jesus. And you start thinking, "God really likes me, but he can't stand those scuzzballs."

Then people who deliberately reject God seem like your *personal* enemies — and the next step is feeling glad that in the end they'll lose. "God will waste you, slime, and I'll love watching every minute of it!" (The ultimate step is to think God needs some help doing the wasting.) But when people who follow the Lord of love begin hating those who are not yet followers, something is royally wrong.

We've stopped much of that. We've said, "Hey, let's remember God loves everybody." True. Good deal.

We've said, "Listen, we can't judge others. We don't know what it's like to be in their shoes. We don't know what makes them tick. Maybe they had a really screwed-up childhood. Judging people is God's business." That's also very true. Another good deal.

And then for some of us comes a huge mistake, a horrible, horrendous cosmic mistake. We figure, "Maybe it doesn't really make any difference how we act. We're probably all just acting the way we're programmed. God will fix everything in the end anyway, so why worry?"

Some of us are trying so hard to avoid being Christian snobs that we forget we have to be different in order to be Christians at all. We're trying so hard not to judge others as sinners that we figure sin itself maybe doesn't make any difference.

And that's fatal.

We can't shut ourselves up in a church and congratulate one

another on how wonderful we are. But we can't just melt and blend into a society that says, "If it feels good, do it" or "If you want it, go for it."

God sees sin (and hates it) separately from sinners (whom God continues to love). You might say that comes naturally for God. It's harder for us. But we have to give it our best shot because that's what Jesus calls us to do...to hate sin and fight it (in ourselves and in others) while loving sinners (ourselves and others), and to do this without feeling superior, without judging.

That's a tough script to follow — but definitely worth it. Read Revelation and check out the ending.

CHAPTER TEN

The Nativity Narratives: Breaking Into History

Scene 1: The city desk of a large metropolitan newspaper. The editor-in-chief has angrily called a reporter named Luke into his office. The editor is not a happy camper.

"What is this stuff?" he explodes, waving a copy of Luke's latest story. "I hired you to be a *reporter,* and instead you hand me...whatever you call this! Now, it's got style — I'll give you that. But it's not reporting. Didn't you ever learn the four W's of good reporting — Who-What-When-Where? The more Who-What-When-Where, the better!"

"Of course, sir. I just thought it was more important to emphasize the 'Who' — and the other W."

"What other W?"

"The 'Why.' "

Scene 2: Same as above, but now the reporter's name is Matthew.

"What is this stuff?" the editor explodes. "I hired you to investigate big-time stories and turn out snappy no-nonsense accounts. Instead you begin with a family history of names nobody can pronounce! And what is this stuff at the end — these three mysterious guys? All you say is they came from the East. Congratulations on the astounding detail! Did you interview these guys at all? Didn't you even get their names?"

"Well, sir, the story illustrates the significance of..."

"Significance! You don't understand, son. We're not in the significance business. We tell people what happened, to whom, when, and where. Facts! Got it?"

Wonder of Wonders

That's what might happen if the birth of Jesus took place today and the evangelists Matthew and Luke, hired to cover the event, turned in the opening chapters of their Gospels.

Of course it's natural to wonder what actually happened that night in Bethlehem and the weeks before and after. When we see films or read stories about the birth of Jesus, we say, "I wonder if it really happened like that." We wish Matthew and Luke had given us more details.

"...on a cold winter's night that was so deep." Was it really cold? How cold?

"...shepherds quake at the sight." How many shepherds were there? What did the angel look like? Did the shepherds have trouble finding the stable? Why doesn't Luke tell us these things?

"...star with royal beauty bright." How big was the star? Didn't anybody besides the Magi see it and wonder what was going on? Why doesn't Matthew let us know?

Our curiosity goes on and on. Were there really animals at the stable keeping the baby Jesus warm with their breath? How long did Mary and Joseph stay at the stable? Didn't the shepherds talk about what had happened and bring crowds of people to see for themselves?

If you want a detailed picture of the birth and infancy of Jesus, the accounts in Matthew and Luke will disappoint you. The details are so few, we wonder why they bothered to write the story at all.

Good question: Why did they?

They were giving *previews,* that's why.

The Bottom Line

It's a little like this. You're watching TV. It's nine o'clock; a new show is about to start. A dramatic voice says something like "Tonight on NBC...the gripping story of a young woman caught between love and a bizarre, savage world she never knew existed!" Then for thirty seconds or so you see clips from several scenes of the TV movie about to start.

From hearing and watching this, you pick up a general idea of the movie you're about to see. It will feature a beautiful (of course) young woman who plans to marry the man of her dreams — until she discovers that he's the leader of a satanic cult that practices gruesome rituals.

That's a preview of the movie's plot. But when you think a little more deeply, you realize it's also a glimpse of the major ideas or themes: conflict of loyalties, reality of the supernatural, and the battle between the powers of good and evil.

That's the kind of preview Matthew and Luke give in the opening chapters of their Gospels: a preview of ideas, the *meaning* of the baby born at Bethlehem. They weren't trying to say, "This is what happened when Jesus was born." They weren't trying to write what the video cameras would have captured on tape if they'd been invented. Matthew and Luke were saying, "This is *who* Jesus is, *why* he came, and *what* that means to us!"

That's the bottom line. If the birth of Jesus means only that we're out of school for a while and hope to get lots of presents, then it doesn't matter whether Jesus was born in a wooden stable or a Styrofoam igloo. It doesn't matter whether there were three wise men or three goofy geezers and six dizzy dopes.

What matters is what Jesus' birth means to human beings — and *that* is what Matthew and Luke are talking about.

Reading the Christmas stories, or "infancy narratives," with this attitude is a surprisingly different experience. Try it! It's like walking along a familiar path that has the same scenery it always did, but the direction and destination of the path are different. Let's sketch two of the main ideas previewed in the infancy narratives.

Breaking and Entering

Monday: ten-question vocabulary quiz; burgers and fries in the cafeteria. Tuesday: double-period chemistry lab; corn dogs and Tater Tots in the cafeteria. Wednesday: first draft of weekly composition due; spaghetti and meatballs in the cafeteria.

And so it goes to the following Monday when we have (surprise!): ten-question vocabulary quiz; burgers and fries in the...

Sometimes it seems as though time is an endlessly repeating cycle of the same or at least very similar things. History re-and-re-and-recycled.

But the Israelites didn't see it that way. To them history was a moving line with a direction, sort of like a train with a destination. And they were right.

Now the Israelites never even thought of time travel, but it's a common idea in modern stories and films like the *Star Trek* series and *Back to the Future* films.

Whenever Captain Kirk and company or Marty McFly and Doc Brown landed in the past, they were careful not to do anything that would change the future. They had a strong sense that it would be wrong to mess with history. It would be like breaking and entering where they had no right to be.

But it's different with God. God is the Lord of history and has every right to break and enter it, to forever change it...especially since he always breaks in and enters history in order to leave special gifts.

That's the idea behind the list of names at the beginning of

Matthew's Gospel. To us, the list is almost meaningless. But it wasn't when Matthew wrote it, and it doesn't have to be for us when we understand it.

Matthew gives us the ancestry of Jesus, a nice orderly list arranged in three sets of fourteen each — with four exceptions. The exceptions are all women; each was a foreigner who unexpectedly "broke into" Israelite history and whose motherhood came about in some exceptional, divinely directed manner. That, of course, sets the stage for Mary's motherhood of Jesus.

Matthew's list of strange names is saying, "History has been leading up to the birth of Jesus from the beginning of time, and whenever things needed a push in the right direction, God reached down into history and gave it that push."

Luke illustrates the same thing in his account of the conception of John the Baptist. Mary's cousin Elizabeth was unable (and too old) to have children. Along comes second cousin John anyway.

And then Jesus. A human mother...fatherhood arranged by the Spirit, the mighty wind (*breath*) of God, the same Spirit-wind-breath who hovered over the waters in the second verse of Genesis, about to make wonderful things happen.

God is in charge, friends and neighbors. Even when it doesn't seem like it; even when things seem pretty ordinary for a long stretch of time; even when things seem to be going wrong. That's the first big preview.

And it implies a mystery we'll never be able to figure out. God is in charge even though he has made us free — free to foul up when we choose wrongly; free to reject him.

That's the story Matthew and Luke are previewing. Jesus — God — came to earth in the greatest act of breaking and entering history ever, and yet the people were free to reject him. In the end some of them handed him the biggest rejection of all — they put him to death. And his death in turn opened the way to our salvation, which is what God had in mind all along.

God breaks into and enters history, leaves us free yet stays in charge. A mystery, for sure. The river of history flows on to the end God has decided. It's our free choice either to go with that flow or to fight it and dash ourselves against the rocks.

And that idea of free choice brings us to the second main idea previewed in the Nativity stories.

For or Against?

Herod was a dingbat. Cruel and evil, yes, but mostly one of the all-time greatest dingbats.

Now along come these three very scholarly, very important men. They've made one heck of a long journey (not easy in those times), guided by a mysterious star that isn't part of the normal skyline, looking for the newborn king.

They arrive in Jerusalem for some final details from Herod. Herod thinks...messiah! The long-awaited savior of the people! The one his people have been hoping for and thinking about and praying about for centuries.

Herod consults with the best minds of the time and asks where the messiah is foretold to be born. Answer: in Bethlehem — about four and a half miles down the road.

Now does that pretty much lock it up or what?

So what does Herod do? Lie. Plot. Scheme. He tries anything to get the messiah, God's heaven-sent savior, out of his life — dead!

Who *does* accept Jesus?

Three guys from far away — three outsiders.

And some shepherds — not exactly the big-time-glitzy high rollers of society back then.

How could Herod and his advisers have been so stupid? It's incredible!

But this is a preview, remember. It kept happening. In spite of all that Jesus did and said and showed and proved, many still turned their backs on him and said, "We can't handle this stuff. We don't need this. Get him out of here."

It still happens. Herod and his advisers and the wise men and the shepherds...they're still hanging around. People you'd least expect — real long shots, even "nonbelievers" — do things to help bring about the peace and harmony that God wants for us. Simple, ordinary, non-glitzy people — nerds and nobodies — live the joy of the gospel.

On the other hand, some people who were brought up with the truth from childhood, who have gotten every religious break, say "We don't need this" to Jesus and try to get him out of their lives.

The next time Christmas rolls around, try this: read the Nativity and infancy stories in Matthew and Luke — not for details of the great event in Bethlehem but for what they are telling you about Jesus.

CONCLUSION

When you finish reading *And Then There Were None,* you've found out who really was committing all those eerie, one-by-one murders on the island. You probably enjoyed the book, but it would be seriously silly to begin reading it again.

When you reach the end of *Great Expectations,* you wonder if Charles Dickens was getting paid by the word, and you're ready to write your English report and take the final test. But even though you've enjoyed finding out what happens to Pip, you'll probably be middle-aged before you feel an urge to pick up the book again.

Chances are you haven't read the Bible or even the New Testament straight through. That's fine because it's not intended to be read that way.

But you *can* pick up the same part of the New Testament, the same gospel or letter, and read it again very soon. If you do (and if you read it in the right setting, as God *suggested* in the Introduction), you'll discover an amazing thing: it doesn't feel like a rerun.

That's because you never reach the bottom or the end of God's Word. The more you read Scripture, the more you see different and deeper meanings in the same verses you read recently.

And that's, well, kind of fun.

Give it a shot.